HISTORY & GEOGRAPHY
MODERN NATIONS
WESTERN EUROPE

CONTENTS

Author: Bess Morton
Editor-in-Chief: Richard W. Wheeler, M.A. Ed.
Editor: Elizabeth Loeks Bouman
Consulting Editor: Howard Stitt, Th.M., Ed.D.
Revision Editor: Alan Christopherson, M.S.

Alpha Omega Publications®

804 N. 2nd Ave. E., Rock Rapids, IA 51246-1759
© MCMXCVI by Alpha Omega Publications, Inc.   All rights reserved.
LIFEPAC is a registered trademark of Alpha Omega Publications, Inc.

MODERN NATIONS I: WESTERN EUROPE

By the end of the thirteenth century, wealthy merchants all over Western Europe had bought great portions of land. These lands once were parts of feudal manors. On them the merchants built large city-states, which they ruled. City life, not rural, became the center of human activity. Busy commerce developed between the cities. You learned about these things in an earlier LIFEPAC®. In this LIFEPAC you will follow events that happened in Western European countries from the time called the Middle Ages until the present time. By the end of the thirteenth century, boundaries of the countries of Europe were defined. Strong national feelings grew. Explorers sailed out in the name of their home countries and conquered lands across the oceans.

At the same time banks were established for the exchange of money. The largest of these became the Medici Bank in Florence, Italy.

Italy is situated between the Near East, on the one hand, and Western Europe on the other. During the early centuries of the Middle Ages, brisk trading with both markets made Italy a rich country. Many people had time to be interested in art and science. A new spirit of wanting to learn came to Italy. A spirit of wanting to be free spread slowly into the whole continent of Europe.

In this period, the Roman Catholic Church lost some of its supremacy. People began to hope God could touch them as individual persons.

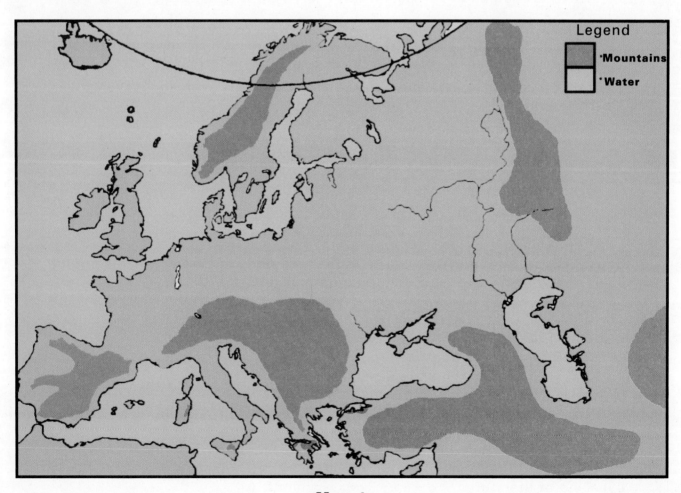

Map 1

You will learn in this LIFEPAC about the Protestant Reformation. Most probably you will begin to know God better yourself.

The study of the Industrial Revolution should help you to appreciate the growth of huge cities. Mass production of goods began as a result of the Industrial Revolution. What happened in the twentieth century would not have been possible without mass production.

Today we live in the "Age of Unrest." Starting in the early 1900s, this time has been marked by two world wars and by money problems. People in some countries lost freedoms they had worked hard to get. This study will help you to understand the need to follow Jesus' teachings carefully.

OBJECTIVES

Read these objectives. The objectives tell you what you should be able to do when you have successfully completed this LIFEPAC.

When you have finished this LIFEPAC, you should be able to:

1. Name at least three areas in which awakening took place in Western Europe during the Renaissance.

2. Tell how a person of Protestant faith seeks God.

3. Describe three inventions that revolutionized the textile industry in England.

4. Name at least three reasons why England was the most involved of all the Western European countries in the Industrial Revolution.

5. State the starting dates and at least two other facts each about World War I and World War II.

6. Describe the Berlin tragedy.

VOCABULARY

Study these new words. Learning the meanings of these words is a good study habit and will improve your understanding of this LIFEPAC.

accelerate (ak sel' u rāt). Increase speed.
adhere (ad hir'). Stick fast.
affable (af' u bul). Easy to approach; courteous.
alliance (a lī' uns). State of being joined together.
apex (ā' peks). The highest point of anything.
architecture (är' ku tek' chur). The designing and drawing of buildings.
blockade (block ād'). Barring entrance or exit to a place.
classical (klas' u kul). Relating in some way to the classics.
classics (klas' iks). Creations of enduring value; perfect specimens, especially speaking of literature.

clergy (kler′ jē). Priests, ministers.

communism (kom′ yu niz um). Political system that advocates state ownership of land and property

corrupt (ku rupt′). Becomes or makes impure, tainted, or injured.

dictatorship (dik tā′ tur ship). Power to give orders that must be obeyed.

diplomacy (di plō′ mu sē). Practice of discussing terms between nations.

dogma (dog′ ma). Formally stated principles of faith taught by the church.

era (ē′ rä). A period of time; a stage of history.

etcher (ech′ ėr). One who engraves on metal, glass, or the like, by means of acid.

extermination (ex stėr mu nā′ shun). Complete destruction.

fascism (fash′ iz um). A strongly nationalistic political theory in favor of government control of industry and labor.

Fascist (fash′ ist). A person who favors and supports fascism.

indulgences (in dul′ jun suz). In the Roman Catholic Church the remission of the punishment still due after the guilt of a sin has been forgiven.

manse (mans). The house assigned to or occupied by a minister.

mural (myủr′ ul). Pertaining to a wall, as a painting on a wall.

national socialism (nash′ u nul sō′ shu liz um). The doctrines of the Nazis, including totalitarian government and state control of industry but opposition to communism.

penitential deeds (pen′ u ten′ shul deedz). In the Roman Catholic Church, acts performed to show one is sorry for a sin.

perceive (pėr sēv′). To apprehend with the mind; understand.

perspective (pėr spek′ tiv). Relative distance and positions as seen by the eye.

psychological (sī kō loj′ u kul). Of or belonging to the mind or to psychology.

psychology (sī kol′ u jē). The science and study of the mind.

realistic (rē′ u lis′ tik). True to life.

shuttle (shut′ ul). To move back and forth.

sociology (sō shē ol′ u jē). The science and study of human groups or society.

spindle (spin′ dul). A device that spins as it turns, especially used for spinning thread.

spire (spīr). A slender, tapering stalk or steeple of a church.

strategy (strat′ u jē). Large-scale military planning.

tactics (tak′ tiks). The science or art of moving troops or ships in action.

textile (teks′ tul). Of or having to do with weaving; cloth.

theologian (thē′ ō lō′ jun). One who studies God.

trustworthy (trust′ wėr thē). Reliable; deserving confidence.

unification (yu ni fi cā′ shun). To form into a whole.

Note: All vocabulary words in this LIFEPAC appear in **boldface** print the first time they are used. If you are unsure of the meaning when you are reading, study the definitions given.

Pronunciation Key: hat, āge, cãre, fär; let, ēqual, tėrm; it, īce; hot, ōpen, ôrder; oil; out; cup, pút, rüle; **ch**ild; lo**ng**; **th**in; /_TH_/ for **th**en; /zh/ for mea**s**ure; /u/ represents /a/ in **a**bout, /e/ in tak**e**n, /i/ in penc**i**l, /o/ in lem**o**n, and /u/ in circ**u**s.

I. THE RENAISSANCE

The word *Renaissance* means rebirth. Renaissance is used to indicate a time of renewal or revival. Many scholars of the early fourteenth century thought that, in order to come out of darkness, the world had to return to the bright days of Rome and Greece. They wanted the **Classical** Age to be reborn. However, they did not entirely return to something old. When an interest in education was revived, men were also awakened to new ways of thinking and doing. The Renaissance saw an awakening in the arts and **architecture**, exploration, religion, and other fields.

SECTION OBJECTIVES

Review these objectives. When you have completed this section, you should be able to:

1. Name at least three areas in which awakening took place in Western Europe during the Renaissance.
2. Tell how a person of Protestant faith seeks God.

Restudy these words.

architecture	etcher	psychology
classical	indulgences	realistic
classics	mural	sociology
clergy	penitential deeds	spire
corrupt	perceive	theologian
dogma	perspective	trustworthy
era		

AWAKENING IN LEARNING

In the early 1300s men began to see new value in the **classical** writings of the early Greeks and Romans. A revival of learning developed. Scholars began to think it was important to free human minds from the errors that had misled them through the Dark Ages and Middle Ages. Many schools were established.

One of the great Italian scholars who studied the **classics** of Greece and Rome was Francesco Petrarch (peet' rark), 1304-1374. Petrarch taught that 1) man was able to reason for himself, 2) man was able to will his own thoughts and behavior, and 3) man could **perceive** problems and solutions for himself.

These ideas are generally accepted today. In the fourteenth century Petrarch's words were like rays of hope because people were used to having someone else tell them what to think and believe.

A century later a scholar named Desiderius Erasmus (ear az' mus), 1469-1536, spoke from Rotterdam in Holland. He disliked the rigid church **dogmas** that were taught in his day. These teachings often were very hard to follow. Persons who disobeyed them usually had to do **penitential deeds** for a long time. Erasmus asked teachers to educate people to think for themselves. Erasmus wanted people to be able to decide to do what was right rather than be forced to do it.

After the start of the Renaissance, philosophers, educators, and **theologians** began to teach more freely. Their work has brought us to the freedom of thought and worship we have in the United States of America now. The modern sciences of **sociology** and **psychology** also have grown out of the thinking of early scholars.

Write *true* **or** *false*.

1.1 _____ Wealthy merchants created huge farms out of the old feudal manors.

1.2 _____ The Medici Bank in Florence was the largest bank in Europe.

1.3 _____ Petrarch thought a man should have a teacher tell him what to think.

1.4 _____ Erasmus believed people should have to live by rigid dogmas.

1.5 _____ The study of psychology grew out of the new freedom of thought in the Renaissance.

1.6 _____ The center of human activity became the city-states.

1.7   Six characteristics of the time between the end of the Middle Ages and the start of the Renaissance were a. _____ , b. _____ , c. _____ , d. _____ , e. _____ , and f. _____ .

1.8   Along with a spirit of wanting to learn, there was a revival of _____ _____ .

1.9   The writings of the early Greeks and Romans are called _____ _____ .

1.10   A theologian is a _____ .

___

AWAKENING IN THE ARTS AND ARCHITECTURE

During the Middle Ages artistic works were controlled by the Roman Catholic Church. All paintings and sculptures were expected to be of religious subjects. Even before the Renaissance came to other fields, art and **architecture** were affected by the rising freedom of thought.

Art. Artists were caught up in the spirit of new freedom. They began to do finer work. Their pictures had better depth and **perspective**. Many famous paintings still can be seen on the walls of churches in Italy and elsewhere. Michelangelo's (1475-1564) **murals** are in the Sistine Chapel of the Vatican in Rome. Vast and sweeping, they combine **realistic** detail with biblical allegory. Michelangelo was also a sculptor and an architect.

Leonardo da Vinci (1452-1519) was another fine painter and sculptor. His Mural, *The Last Supper,* has inspired Christians everywhere. This picture is still in Milan, Italy, but because he used experimental paints, the picture is fading from the church wall.

Though the largest number of Renaissance artists came from Italy, good painters arose everywhere in Western Europe. Among those good painters were Dürer, Brueghel the Elder, and El Greco. Dürer, (doo' rer) (1471-1528) was a famous German **etcher** and painter. Brueghel (brew' gul) the Elder (1520-1569) was Flemish. His two sons, who followed him as painters, worked in Belgium also. El Greco (gray' co) (1548-1614) was born in Crete, but lived most of his life in Spain. Besides paintings and sculptures, artists worked on etchings, woodcuts, and other forms of craftsmanship.

Artists no longer confined their work to religious subjects. Their paintings and statues began to express the life of the people.

Gothic Church
with spires pointing to heaven

Bramante's Tempietto
Lowered roofline symbolized God close to man.

Architecture. The Gothic cathedrals of the Middle Ages had high **spires** pointing to heaven and God. Inside, their ceilings were high. During the Renaissance, architects such as Donato Bramante (braum aun' tay) (1444-1514), Michelangelo, Da Vinci, and others all lowered the steeples and interiors of churches they designed. Their purpose was to make men have the feeling of the love of God surrounding them.

Complete the statements.

In this LIFEPAC you are given the dates when some of the persons were born and when they died. Dates are handy tools to use to place the persons in proper times and places. Dates also help us to know how long a person lived, or how old he was when a certain event happened.

1.11   By looking at Michelangelo's dates we can tell that he lived to be
_____ years old.

1.12   Leonardo Da Vinci lived for _____ years.

1.13   We can tell Michelangelo and Da Vinci possibly knew each other because their names are both Italian and their _____ overlap.

1.14   Leonardo Da Vinci was _____ (older, younger) than
        Michelangelo.
1.15   Leonardo Da Vinci was _____ years old when
        Michelangelo was born.
1.16   We know El Greco never knew Dürer personally because _____
        _____ .
1.17   Dürer died when Brueghel was only _____ years old.
1.18   Bramante died five years before _____ .

Write *true* **or** *false.*

1.19   _____   Renaissance artists did poor work.
1.20   _____   The ceilings of Renaissance churches were lower than those of Gothic
                   churches.
1.21   _____   Brueghel the Elder was an Italian artist.
1.22   _____   Da Vinci's mural, *The Last Supper*, has been preserved in a museum.
1.23   _____   Besides being a painter, Michelangelo is well known for his sculptures.
1.24   _____   All Renaissance paintings are of religious subjects.

AWAKENING IN EXPLORATION

If we, in the United States, know how and why our continent was discovered, we can understand why we still have close ties to Western Europe. It is exciting to relive in imagination those explorations with the brave men who dared to do them. The European discoverers of Renaissance times mainly sought westerly trade routes by water to India and the Orient.

Columbus. Christopher Columbus was a Renaissance explorer. He was certain that if he could sail westward in the Atlantic Ocean, he could reach the Far East. This route would be faster and easier than a water route around the coast of Africa, or so he thought. He believed the earth was round, but, of course, he had no idea how long the earth's circumference was. When he was about thirty years old he tried to persuade the king of Portugal to finance sailors and ships to carry out his voyage plan. The king of Portugal refused him.

King Ferdinand and Queen Isabella of Spain finally consented to send him. They outfitted him with three ships and less than a hundred men. Columbus and these men left Spain August 3, 1492, in three small ships. The journey took weeks of sailing with no land in sight—nothing but ocean water. His men almost mutinied. Finally land was sighted. On October 12 the men set foot on shore of San Salvador Island (now Watling's Island) in the Bahamas.

After that the rulers of Spain gave him more ships and more men. Columbus made three more trips to the New World. Once he sailed past the north coast of South America. He believed, all the time, he was viewing islands off the mainland of India.

After Columbus, a steady stream of explorers sailed westward to the new land. Mainly they came from Portugal, Spain, England, and Italy. Each established colonies in the name of his country. Some colonies were founded in North America, some in South America.

World-wide explorers. One Portuguese navigator named Vasco da Gama did find a water route to India. He sailed around the south coast of Africa and into the Indian Ocean in 1497.

In the year 1500 Pedro Alvarez Cabral was sent out by Portugal to follow the same route to India that Vasco da Gama discovered. His fleet sailed too far west so that his expedition discovered Brazil, in South America, by accident. Eventually getting back on course, Cabral reached India. He established a factory there before returning home.

Ferdinand Magellan also flew the flag of Portugal. His fleet was the first to sail around the world. In 1519 he was given five ships. In your study of South America you learned how he had trouble with his men at Patagonia in Argentina. He managed to get through the strait at the southern tip of South America. From there his ships (now only four because of the Patagonia mutiny) took ninety-eight days to sail to the Far East. Magellan and his men named the western ocean the *Pacific*, because of its gentle winds and calm seas. The voyage was barely endurable. The ships had no fresh provisions, little water, and spoiled bread. The men resorted to eating oxhides, sawdust, and rats. Scurvy, a disease of the skin, afflicted them all.

In March of 1521, Magellan's fleet reached the Philippine Islands. A month and a half later Magellan was killed by natives. Later one of his ships, the Victoria, made it home to Portugal. A crew member acting as captain brought the ship back around the coast of Africa. The fact that the trip was completed meant that a new **era** in worldwide travel had begun. More importantly, men now knew how far it was to the Orient, and that unexplored continents lay in between.

 **Answer these questions in complete sentences.**

1.25 What was the main purpose of the Renaissance explorers?

_____

_____

1.26 Why did Columbus sail west when he wanted to reach the Far East?

_____

_____

1.27   How was a water route to India found? _____

_____

1.28   Which fleet was the first to sail around the world? _____

_____

AWAKENING IN RELIGION

At the time of the awakening, the Roman Catholic Church had many good people in it. Some of the **clergy**, however, had **corrupted** the practices of the church. Erasmus, Luther, Calvin, and John Knox are the most well-known of those who tried to reform and renew the Christian church.

Reformation attempts within the church. Many Catholic scholars, like Erasmus, thought the Roman Catholic Church's demands were unnecessarily strict. Also, a general feeling had grown that the practice of selling **indulgences** rather than assigning penitential deeds was harmful. Several leaders within the Roman Catholic Church tried to change the church's ways. Their efforts were not altogether successful.

Martin Luther was a Catholic priest who, more and more, disagreed with some of the teachings and practices of his church. He was a strong German man, very sensitive and emotional. Often he became discouraged.

In 1517 he was reading in the New Testament and became convinced he should declare his objections to his church. He wrote down ninety-five theses (reasons) why he thought the Roman Catholic Church was wrong. He nailed the theses to the door of the castle church in Wittenberg. Read in your Bible Romans 1:16 and 17. These are the words that changed Martin Luther's life.

Protestant Reformation. Luther soon left the Roman Catholic Church. He preached that people may approach God directly for salvation. He preached that if a person prays for forgiveness he will receive God's forgiveness directly. He preached this message to the end of his days. His followers are called Lutherans.

Because of the protests of Luther and others against corrupt practices within the church, these people were called Protestants. The term, Protestant church, had its beginning in these events.

Protestant services have always been in the language of the people. The Gutenberg press had been invented about sixty years before Luther started his work. Bibles were being printed in increasing quantity. Luther taught the people to read the Scriptures for themselves. Luther believed the Holy Spirit would guide them to understand the words they were reading. We believe this, too.

Lutheranism spread mainly to the countries of Scandinavia. These countries have the same Germanic roots in custom and language that Germany has.

Luther's teachings were a revival of first century Christianity. These teachings were responsible for a new spiritual awakening all over Europe. The awakening led to reformation, that is, the reforming of the church.

A reformer of Luther's time was a man named John Calvin, a theologian who taught in Geneva, Switzerland. The church he founded was called the Reformed Church. A little less stern than the Lutheran Church, the Reformed Church spread quickly to Holland and across all of Central Europe including France. The Protestants in France were called Huguenots.

In Great Britain, reformation started in Scotland. The leader in Scotland was John Knox. His followers later formed the Presbyterian congregations.

The Church of England, or Episcopal Church, was started for political reasons, not religious reasons, during the reign of Henry VIII in the mid 1500s. The Church of England became a full-fledged Protestant church toward the end of the century.

Religious fervor for reform led to the establishment of many other denominations during the Renaissance period.

 Complete this activity.

Some of the following words are found in the section *Awakening in Religion*. Each of them has a prefix. On the left is the word, to the right an explanation of the prefix and definition of the total word.

Now do these four things.
1. Read the word.
2. Read the explanations to the right.
3. Under the word to the left put 1 line under the prefix.
4. Under the word to the left put 2 lines under the root word.

	Word	Prefix Explanation	Word Definition With Prefix
1.29	a. reform	*re-* = again	to form again
	b. revival	*re-* = again	re+*vivere* (to live) to live again
	c. remain	*re-* = back	re+*manere* (to stay) to stay back
1.30	a. unnecessary	*un-* = no or not	not necessary
	b. denomination	*de-* = to intensify	de+*nomen* (name) to put all of one name together
	c. demand	*de-* = to intensify	de+*mandate* (command) to make a mandate stronger
	d. awake	*a-* = to intensify	to intensify the wakened state

11

	Word	Prefix Explanation	Word Definition With Prefix
1.31	became	*be-* = affect with	came to be
1.32	forgiveness	*for-* = opposite or away	the act of giving away any fine that might be given. (To refuse to give a fine.)
1.33	a. include	*in-* = in, into, within	in+*claudere* (to shut) to shut within
	b. important	*im-* = within	im+*portare* (to carry, a message) = within the value of the message
	c. individual	*in-* = not	in+*divide* = not divisible

Match the following names and phrases.

1.34	_____	Erasmus
1.35	_____	John Knox
1.36	_____	Calvin
1.37	_____	Wittenberg
1.38	_____	Luther
1.39	_____	Geneva
1.40	_____	Huguenots
1.41	_____	Henry VIII

a. the Christian church
b. French Protestants
c. city in which the ninety-five theses were nailed to the door of the castle church
d. established the Church of England for political reasons
e. the Reformed Church began here
f. the Scottish reformer
g. a German priest who finally left the Roman Catholic Church
h. a Catholic scholar who tried to change the Roman Catholic Church
i. Swiss theologian

AWAKENING IN OTHER FIELDS

The sense of personal worth brought by the Renaissance led men to creative goals in just about every area of life. Changes in music prepared the way for the composers of classical music, such as Bach and Handel. Classical music, however, came after the Renaissance period. When you read the following paragraphs, you will realize the work of men during the awakening still has a strong effect on our everyday lives.

Science. Copernicus (ko pur′ nee kus), 1473-1543, from Poland, was the first great astronomer of the new age.

In 1608, Hans Lippershey, a Dutchman, followed Copernicus with the invention of the telescope. His telescope helped men to observe the sky and the movements of the heavenly bodies.

These men are only two of the many men who began to work in scientific fields during the Renaissance. You will read about others in different LIFEPACs. One important fact to remember is the careful way they all recorded their information and conclusions. This careful recording has resulted in the scientific method of research. All **trustworthy** scientists use this method to gain and to store knowledge.

Government. Toward the end of the Middle Ages, at Runnymede, outside of London, England, King John was forced to sign a document called the *Magna Carta* (the Great Charter). Certain rights and privileges to his people were guaranteed by the king.

After the Great Charter, the movement toward more freedom through government became stronger. The belief grew that all men are equal under God, capable of governing themselves. This idea was not new. Classical Athens and Sparta in Greece were, for a time, governed by the people. Before the Renaissance was over, solid foundations had been laid for later, strong democracies in America and in Western Europe.

Inventions. Leonardo da Vinci, besides being an artist, was an inventor. From thinking up devices to help man float on water, to sketching how to fly like a bat, his active mind kept working. In the mid 1400s Johann Gutenberg invented the printing press. Others claimed to be the first to invent printing. These men paved the way for a succession of inventions. You will learn more about them in the section on the Industrial Revolution.

Complete these activities.

1.42 Name the procedure that trustworthy scientists use to gain and store knowledge. _____

1.43 Name Lippershey's important invention. _____

1.44 Name the two cities of ancient Greece which had government by the people. _____

1.45 Name the king of England who was forced to sign the Great Charter.

_____

1.46 Name two of Leonardo da Vinci's inventive ideas.
   a. _____
   b. _____

Write a paragraph.

1.47   In your opinion which of the awakenings studied in this section (learning, arts and architecture, exploration, religion, science, government, or invention) did more to influence life in the United States where you live today? Write a paragraph giving reasons for your answer. _____

_____

_____

_____

_____

_____

_____

_____

_____

_____

_____

_____

Teacher check _____

                                 Initial   Date

 **Complete this map activity.**

    Use Map 3 on page 36 to find the countries in which the following cities are located. Underline them in red on the map and write the names of the countries in the blanks.

1.48 _____ Florence

1.49 _____ Wittenberg

1.50 _____ London

1.51 _____ Rome

1.52 _____ Geneva

1.53 _____ Edinburgh

1.54 _____ Rotterdam

1.55 _____ Milan

SELF TEST 1

Write *true* **or** *false* (each answer, 2 points).

1.01 _____ The classical period was centered in ancient Palestine.
1.02 _____ Michelangelo sketched plans for a way for men to fly.
1.03 _____ *Awakening* in this LIFEPAC refers to the Renaissance.
1.04 _____ *Renaissance* means *revival*.
1.05 _____ Many scholars recommended returning to the classics.
1.06 _____ Freedom of thought keeps us from doing well in school.
1.07 _____ Petrarch thought man could will his thoughts and behavior.
1.08 _____ Erasmus liked rigid dogmas.
1.09 _____ Florence is in Italy.
1.010 _____ Wittenberg is in Scotland.

Write the correct letter and word or phrase on the line (each answer, 2 points).

1.011   In the Middle Ages all art was about _____ .
           a. religious subjects   c. landscapes
           b. icons   d. family life

1.012   Leonardo da Vinci painted _____ .
           a. *The Blue Boy*   c. *The Last Supper*
           b. *The Sistine Chapel*   d. *The Nativity*

1.013   Renaissance artists began to depict the _____ .
           a. life of the people   c. country roads
           b. church life   d. life in the city-states

1.014   Michelangelo was a _____ .
           a. painter and sculptor   c. priest and author
           b. sailor and explorer   d. merchant and trader

1.015   Renaissance architects lowered their church steeples and interior ceilings to _____ .
           a. make them easier to build
           b. save on building materials
           c. make men feel the love of God close to them
           d. make them easier to heat

1.016   Columbus sailed in the name of _____ .
        a. Spain   c. England
        b. Portugal   d. Italy

1.017   Columbus was an explorer of the _____ .
        a. Middle Ages   c. classical period
        b. Renaissance period   d. Reformation

1.018   Columbus first landed on _____ .
        a. Florida   c. Newfoundland
        b. South America   d. San Salvador Island

1.019   A ship from Magellan's fleet was _____ .
        a. sunk in the Pacific Ocean   c. first to go around Africa
        b. first to go around the world   d. lost

1.020   The explorer who discovered Brazil by mistake was _____ .
        a. Cabot   c. Cabral
        b. Vasco da Gama   d. Magellan

Match these words and phrases (each answer, 2 points).

1.021 _____ Roman Catholic   a. Church of England
1.022 _____ Martin Luther   b. Reformed Church
1.023 _____ indulgences   c. castle church at Wittenberg
1.024 _____ ninety-five theses   d. permission not to do penitential
1.025 _____ John Calvin   deeds
1.026 _____ individual person   e. Presbyterians
1.027 _____ John Knox   f. Lutheran
1.028 _____ Gutenberg press   g. philosophers
1.029 _____ Henry VIII   h. Protestant belief
1.030 _____ Huguenots   i. French Protestants
                                 j. Bibles
                                 k. penitential deeds

Complete these statements (each answer, 3 points).

1.031   Classics, as referred to by scholars of the Renaissance, were written by
        _____ .

1.032   City-states of the Renaissance were once _____ .

1.033   The bank that grew to be the largest was _____ .

1.034   The rulers of the city-states usually were _____
        _____ .

1.035   Lippershey invented the _____ .

1.036   During the Renaissance, when the boundaries for countries were strengthened, there developed _____ .

1.037   The scientific method is used for research by _____

_____ .

1.038   The early document that started people thinking about more freedom through government was the _____

_____ .

1.039   The first country that had rule by the people was _____ .

1.040   The first printing press usually is credited to _____ .

Complete these activities (each answer, 5 points).

1.041   Name three areas in which awakening took place during the Renaissance.

a. _____

b. _____

c. _____

1.042   Tell how a person of the Protestant faith finds salvation. _____

_____

_____

Possible Score   100

My Score   _____

Teacher check   _____

Initial   Date

II. THE INDUSTRIAL REVOLUTION

The Renaissance period generally is considered to have closed at the end of the sixteenth century. During the next hundred years Western European growth was quiet but steady. Portugal and Spain sent explorers and colonists to South America, Mexico, and what is now the western United States. World trade routes were strengthened in spite of pirates that roamed the seas. A number of French people, traders and Huguenots, made permanent villages in Canada. Pilgrims and Puritans, and other settlers from England, landed on the east coast of North America. Jamestown, the first white settlement in the new land, and Plymouth Rock, where the Mayflower landed, are familiar names to all Americans. Many of the pioneers came in search of religious freedom.

In Europe and elsewhere political conflict grew in the public mind. On one hand, citizens hated to give up heartfelt allegiance to their kings, queens, and princes. On the other, the feeling was growing stronger that the people should have a voice in their own government.

At the same time, men were making machines that were more and more complex. The populations of Western Europe were growing. Easier and better ways to do simple tasks were needed to meet new demands.

By the beginning of the eighteenth century, Western Europe entered a new age, the Industrial Revolution. This revolution was not fought with guns. The Industrial Revolution was a change from making things one at a time by hand to making them hundreds at a time by machines. The Industrial Revolution grew out of the new freedoms brought on by the awakening, or Renaissance. The awakening changed the lives of people; therefore, it was a revolution.

City life, as known today, had its beginning during this period. The study of the Industrial Revolution should be of real interest to you.

SECTION OBJECTIVES

Review these objectives. When you have completed this section, you should be able to:

3. Describe three inventions that revolutionized the textile industry in England.
4. Name at least three reasons why England was the most involved of all the countries of all the Western European countries in the Industrial Revolution.

Restudy these words.

accelerate	manse	spindle
affable	shuttle	textile

CONTRIBUTING FACTORS

The new colonies in America and the Far East made larger demands on European factories for goods and services. The new colonies in turn provided sources for added raw materials. Brisk trading resulted.

Up to the 1700s water power, or wood charcoal power, was used in manufacturing. This meant **textile** factories had to be located by a river or deep stream. Iron factories needed to be within hauling distance of forests. Only near the forests could enough charcoal be made from the wood to keep the furnaces going. Coal, steam, and electric power were the new sources of energy that were needed by new inventions.

Coal. The discovery of coal as a fuel for blast furnaces in factories revolutionized the manufacture of iron products. Most iron industries could then be put in areas where coal was abundant. In England this area was called the "black country." Coal was black, of course. Also the smoke from coal furnaces was black. It colored the buildings and streets. The very air of factory cities became dark from soot.

Steam Power. Later, in about 1769, James Watt greatly improved the steam-powered engine. This improvement made large changes in the textile industries, both cotton and wool. Textile factories moved away from rivers and streams. They could now be located in any convenient place.

Demand for cotton goods became so widespread that much more cotton needed to be grown. Many farms grew up in the West Indies. Eventually, in the United States, Eli Whitney invented the cotton gin to remove seeds from the cotton bolls. America then became a major source for cotton.

After steam power was discovered, inventions seemed to come at a rapid rate. Major accomplishments were achieved in the field of travel. Steam locomotives for railway cars and ships speeded up the shipment of goods by land and sea.

Electric power. Do you remember the story of Benjamin Franklin and his kite during a storm? Sometime after Franklin's discovery of the principle of electricity, electricity began to be used as a source for industrial power. Manufacturing trades in England were now boosted to their highest capabilities.

Write *true* **or** *false.*

2.1 _____ The Renaissance period ended in the twentieth century.

2.2 _____ Many pioneering colonists sought religious freedom.

2.3 _____ New rifles, manufactured in England, were used in the Industrial Revolution.

2.4 _____ The name, Industrial Revolution, means far reaching changes in methods used in manufacturing.

2.5 _____ Population in Western Europe was getting more scarce.

2.6 _____ Strong national feelings means people become proud of and loyal to their own countries.

2.7 _____ French traders and Huguenots made permanent villages in Canada.

2.8 _____ City life as we know it began as a result of the Industrial Revolution.

2.9 _____ The Industrial Revolution changed the lives of people.

2.10 _____ Spain sent no explorers or colonists to the North American continent.

➤ **Write the correct answer on each line.**

2.11 As long as a. _____ power was used in manufacturing,
b. _____ had to be located near wooded areas.

2.12 Factories using water power had to be located along a. _____
and b. _____ .

2.13 The discovery of coal for blast a. _____ changed
completely the methods for manufacturing b. _____
products.

2.14 Coal made good fuel, but streets, walls, and the air in the cities were
filled with a. _____ from b. _____
smoke.

2.15 Coal country was called _____ .

2.16 The steam-powered engine was greatly improved by _____
_____ .

2.17 After the invention of steam-powered engines, textile factories could be
built in _____ places.

2.18 The cotton gin was invented by a. _____ of
the b. _____ .

2.19 America became a major source to England of _____ .

2.20 Steam was also used for railroad a. _____
and b. _____ .

ENGLAND AND
THE INDUSTRIAL REVOLUTION

In a sense all countries of the world were affected by the Industrial Revolution. However, the countries that were most affected by the **acceleration** of industry were (1) France (Before its revolution in 1792, France had ample wood for charcoal. However, it had too little coal to compete in later years.), (2) Germany, (3) Belgium, (4) United States of America, and (5) England. You will learn that England was especially ready for this period of history, and you will learn some of the things it accomplished. You will also learn that England had many problems growing out of the Industrial Revolution.

Advantages. England had enough natural resources, such as coal, to carry on a large amount of industry. Extensive trade routes were established, and the country's navy was strong enough to back them up. The American colonies of England were rebellious, although they remained more stable than the colonies of

20

other countries. A good attitude existed internally in England. Therefore, England became the center of the Western European Industrial Revolution.

Major industry. England's major industry was the manufacture of textiles. Both wool and cotton products were made. In 1835 Britain exported 60 per cent of all cotton goods to the whole world.

However, these strides could not have been made without three inventions. Before discussing the three inventions, the spinning of yarn should be reviewed. You will remember from your study of Bolivia how the women carried **spindles** with them to make yarn out of wool. Look at the illustration.

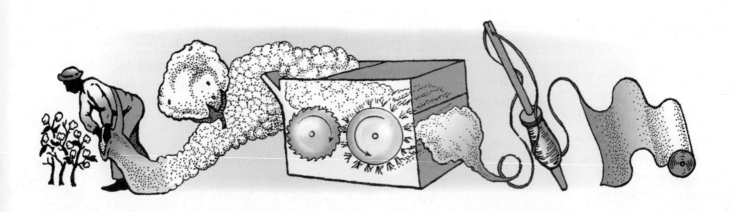

The picture shows the bamboo and wood spindle that was used until the eighteenth century, even for commercial yarn or thread making. The raw material was attached to the small end of the spindle. Then, while turning the spindle quickly, the raw cotton or wool was pulled gently. The faster the whirl, the better the thread spun out.

The spinning wheel was a small improvement. Our colonial grandmothers usually had one of these. A woman could sit by the spinning wheel and operate it with her foot. A pulley would turn the spindle a little faster than by hand.

Either way the yarn or thread could not be produced fast enough. People wanted more thread and fabrics than workers had time to supply.

During the Industrial Revolution the spinning jenny, the roller spinning frame, and the flying shuttle were invented. These three inventions were sorely needed for mass production of textiles.

The spinning jenny could spin hundreds of threads on separate spindles at one time. The roller spinning frame pulled, twisted, and spooled all these separate threads at the same time.

One important part of textile manufacture is the weaving of the yarn or thread into cloth. For years men and women sat at weaving looms with the warp (up and down) threads already strung. The worker used a hand **shuttle** to pass the woof (across) threads back and forth through the warp to make fine cloth. Perhaps you have seen a home weaver or an Indian woman weave rugs in this manner; it takes time to accomplish even a small piece.

Another inventor in England produced the powered flying shuttle. This invention carried the woof through the warp quickly. The process of weaving any type of thread or yarn became very fast. Soon, bolts of cloth were being shipped to markets in every part of the world.

Side effects. As soon as trade picked up, England found it necessary to improve its roads. Huge projects of canal deepening and widening began. Soon, boats from the ocean could go inland, often as far as the factories, to pick up export goods.

A new profession—mechanical engineering—grew out of the inventive spirit of the Industrial Revolution. People who go into this field learn to design machines.

As power methods improved, new industries came into being. Steel manufacture became important in England and in the United States. Many chemical manufacturing plants were developed. These plants used by-products from other industries.

Social problems. The Industrial Revolution brought a better way of life to many. People could buy more good products at lower cost. Factories created jobs for poor people. The business of the cities often stirred up enthusiasm. Some peasants saved the money they earned, invested it, and became rich. Such success stories tended to create false optimism. Great changes brought problems with them, especially in England.

Industries were usually built where farms had been. Much of the old rural life of England was destroyed.

Farmers and peasants moved to cities that were not prepared for them. The cities had been none too clean before the people came. Now they became crowded, ugly, and filthy. It was not until 1848 that a Public Health Act was passed in Britain. Until then garbage, dishwater, and other messes were thrown into the streets. Often a bucketful from an upstairs window caught a passerby below. Charles Dickens,

HISTORY & GEOGRAPHY

608

LIFEPAC TEST

80 / 100

Name _____

Date _____

Score _____

HISTORY & GEOGRAPHY 608: LIFEPAC TEST

Write the correct answer on each line (each answer, 3 points).

1.   *Renaissance* means _____ .

2.   The first Western European attempt at democratic government was the
      _____ .

3.   *Blitzkrieg* means _____ .

4.   Greece and Rome were centers for the _____ .

5.   World War I started with the assassination of Archduke _____
      _____ .

6.   In order to spin yarn or thread, one must have a _____
      _____ .

7.   The man who started the Protestant Reformation was _____
      _____ .

8.   The first ship that went around the world was a ship from
      _____ fleet.

9.   The man who wrote *Mein Kampff* was _____ .

10.   Steam power opened the way for many new _____ .

Match the words and phrases (each answer, 2 points).

11.   _____ Michelangelo   a. Brazil

12.   _____ classics   b. thought the church was too rigid

13.   _____ renewal   c. paintings and architecture

14.   _____ Leonardo da Vinci   d. 1492

15.   _____ Erasmus   e. Greece and Rome

16.   _____ Cabral   f. ninety-five theses

17.   _____ Martin Luther   g. Nazi

18.   _____ castle church   h. Renaissance

19.   _____ Christopher Columbus   i. southern Europe

20.   _____ Italy   j. how to float on water

                                        k. Protestant Reformation

Write the letter and answer on the line (each answer, 2 points).

21. The Magna Carta was a document that _____

    _____ .
    a. freed the slaves
    b. gave the English people a voice in government
    c. described a horse-drawn cart

22. The first printing press was made by _____ .
    a. Eli Whitney
    b. Johann Gutenberg
    c. Leonardo da Vinci

23. Cotton gins _____ .
    a. comb the cotton
    b. spin the cotton
    c. take out the seeds

24. To manufacture textiles after spinning the thread, it is necessary to

    _____ .
    a. knit the thread
    b. wind the thread
    c. weave the thread

25. The manufacture of iron products needed _____ for fuel.
    a. charcoal
    b. coal
    c. wood

26. The method used by scientists to gain and store knowledge is _____

    _____ .
    a. the scientific method
    b. the British method
    c. Leonardo da Vinci

27. During the Industrial Revolution in England, factories were often built

    _____ .
    a. on rivers
    b. on farms
    c. in cities

28. The Renaissance scholar who brought back the idea that man should think for
    himself was _____ .
    a. Michelangelo
    b. Petrarch
    c. Erasmus

29. The Communists started in _____ .
    a. Russia
    b. Germany
    c. Italy

30. Hitler became dictator with the help of the _____ .
    a. Nazi party
    b. Communist Party
    c. Fascist Party

Write *true* **or** *false* (each answer, 2 points).

31. _____ Rural life in England was changed because of the Industrial Revolution.

32. _____ During the Industrial Revolution children were expected to work the same long hours adults did.

33. _____ Before World War I started, Austria-Hungary was wary of Serbia because of border disputes.

34. _____ In anti-aircraft action in World War I, pilots often employed the flying shuttle.

35. _____ Adolf Hitler succeeded Lenin in Russia.

36. _____ France and England declared war to stop Germany's aggressions.

37. _____ The United States joined World War II after Japan attacked Pearl Harbor.

38. _____ Berlin had a free section (or sector) even though it was deep in communist territory.

39. _____ In Europe there were two Germanys.

40. _____ John Wesley lived during the Renaissance.

Answer these questions in complete sentences (each answer, 5 points).

41. What were two of the reasons for World War I?
    a. _____
    _____
    b. _____
    _____

42. In your own words, how may a Christian approach God? _____
_____
_____

the famous British novelist, included descriptions of factory city conditions in his novels.

Factory workers of all ages worked long hours and long weeks. Factory owners hired children to work the same hours as adults.

Gradually, labor unions were formed. The unions helped to gain better working conditions. They began to protect the small children, who often died of overwork. Laws were passed to rid England of some of the bad side effects of manufacturing.

Answer these questions.

2.21 Which country was the center of Western Europe's Industrial Revolution? _____

2.22 What was England's major industry? _____

2.23 What were the three inventions that revolutionized England's textile industry and what did they do?

a. _____

_____

b. _____

_____

c. _____

_____

2.24 What two things did England find it necessary to improve?

a. _____

b. _____

2.25 What happened to rural life when factories were built? _____

_____

2.26 Who worked in the factories? _____

Some Christian answers. John and Charles Wesley were the fifteenth and eighteenth children of a Church of England minister, Samuel Wesley. Both the brothers trained at Oxford University to become Church of England ministers.

When John was a small child, he was barely rescued when the **manse** was consumed by fire. His mother declared him to be a "brand plucked from the burning." From then on she gave him special teaching. She believed John had been saved for a purpose.

However, John Wesley had problems. He was only five feet four inches tall, and his health was poor. In college the religious group he and Charles established was ridiculed. Their church eventually barred them. The Church of England did not like the Wesley methods of religious practice.

John came to America to preach, but his mission here was a failure and he returned to England. Dissatisfied with his own religious life, one evening he attended a small prayer meeting in England. While he was praying he felt his "heart strangely warmed. I felt I did trust Christ...alone...."

This redeeming experience changed his life. He started preaching in fields or lots, wherever anyone would hear him.

Charles Wesley had a similar religious experience at another place and another time. Some of the finest hymns that have ever been written were composed by Charles Wesley.

John Wesley lived and worked in England about the same period of time as the American Revolution. He always traveled on horseback, reading a book. He preached as many as seventeen sermons in one day. Angry crowds were calmed. He seemed to be able to face up to them. To his converts and to ministers he was **affable** and friendly. He was ill, however. Many times he had to jump off his horse into icy waters to stop the bleeding from his nose and throat. Nevertheless, he lived to be almost ninety years old. His message? Only that men, women, and children should seek, and find, salvation through Jesus Christ. He wanted them to experience what he had experienced that night in the prayer meeting. His followers formed the Methodist Church.

Historians say the work of the Wesleys was important. The bad effects of the Industrial Revolution in England could have been much worse except for the work of the Wesleys. A large mass of people had learned of the love of God, and had accepted it, through the Wesley teachings. Faith and hope were common words and attitudes. Many of the new Christians became aware of conditions around them and took steps to improve them.

In Gloucester, England, the publisher, Robert Raikes, started a "Ragged School" in 1780. Robert Raikes was concerned for the children who worked in the factories six days a week. He started a school for them on Sundays. Raikes taught the children reading, writing, and the principles of religion. Raikes gave the idea of "Sunday schools" publicity in his newspaper. Soon Sunday schools were started in factory districts all over England. The idea spread throughout the world. When children no longer worked but went to school, the need to teach reading and writing no longer existed. Sunday schools remained, however, as a means of teaching the principles of religion to children.

Lasting effects. In some ways, the Industrial Revolution continues. New and more efficient machines are still invented. Business has grown today to huge proportions, but factory employees generally have good working conditions. Pollution from manufacturing still exists, but studies are being done to determine how to improve these conditions. Compared to the eighteenth- and nineteenth-century cities, twentieth-century cities are clean.

At the beginning of the twentieth century, however, there remained some of the problems that grew from rapid industry growth. These problems have led to an age of unrest.

Answer these questions.

2.27   What did Robert Raikes do for the working children of England?

_____

2.28   What did John Wesley do for England? _____

_____

_____

2.29   In your own words describe at least three factors that contributed to the Industrial Revolution. Explain how these factors were important.

_____
_____
_____
_____
_____
_____
_____
_____
_____
_____
_____
_____

Teacher check _____

                                   Initial   Date

Complete this atlas study.

2.30   Use an atlas or any map of the British Isles you have available. Mark on Map 2 the following items.

a. Atlantic Ocean
b. English Channel
c. Dover Strait
d. North Channel
e. St. George's Channel
f. Shannon River in Ireland
g. Thames River in England
h. Irish Sea

i. England
j. Scotland
k. Wales
l. North Ireland
m. Irish Republic
n. London
o. Isle of Man

Look at Map 3 on page 36 of this LIFEPAC to see how this portion fits into the total map of Western Europe

Map 2

Complete this atlas study.

Find the cities mentioned in Section II and mark them on Map 2.
Write the name of the country on the blank.

2.31 _____ Oxford

2.32 _____ Gloucester

Complete this reading activity.

Often we can tell what a story is going to be like by reading the first
two or three sentences. The following activities are starting sentences
for six made-up stories. From the Word Bank choose the adjective that
best describes the kind of story each will be. Place the letter in the
proper place.

WORD BANK

a. sad	c. mystery	e. ghost
b. happy	d. combat	f. cruel

2.33 _____   "Not much of a clue," growled Oxnard, sniffing at the apple core.

"Now look," Paula exclaimed, "that happens to be a Rome Beauty apple, not a Delicious...."

The detective sniffed again, "So it is, hmmm- and the only man foolish enough to raise Romes around here is...."

2.34 _____   Martha took two handkerchiefs from her purse. One she handed to Mother. Who could believe the baby lying there had been laughing a moment before!

2.35 _____   Peggy was shaking, her eyes blinking. The soup bowl on the table rattled, with no one near it. Outside the wind whined, but the wail (upstairs, was it?) definitely was not part of the wind.

2.36 _____   John started to snicker, then Peter giggled. From behind the doorway they watched Dad tangle himself further in the string of lights.

"So this is Santa Claus!" the boys shouted, rolling on the floor with laughter.

2.37 _____   The sailor dropped from the helicopter into the foxhole. Boom! Ground six feet away flew apart when the shell hit.

"You land lubbers really get shot at?" gasped the sailor nervously.

2.38 _____   Snatching a piece of heavy sail rope, the ship's master sneered as he lashed it across the boy's bony back. The boy stood straight while the master lashed again. Dropping the rope, the man shook his fist near the boy's mouth, "I'll teach you, I'll teach you to steal a slice of my bread."

Review the material in this section to prepare for the Self Test. The Self Test will check your understanding of this section and will review the first section. Any items you miss on this test will show you what areas you need to restudy.

SELF TEST 2

Match the following words and phrases (each answer, 2 points).

2.01 _____ eighteenth century   a. destroyed by factories
2.02 _____ new colonies   b. new sources of raw materials
2.03 _____ black country   c. hymns
2.04 _____ spinning jenny   d. Industrial Revolution began
2.05 _____ Methodist   e. John Wesley
2.06 _____ Charles Wesley   f. making machines out of machines
2.07 _____ rural life   g. coal country
2.08 _____ filthy   h. steam-powered engine
2.09 _____ James Watt   i. many spindles
2.010 _____ flying shuttle   j. woof threads
                                          k. factory cities

Write the correct letter and answer on the line (each answer, 2 points).

2.011   In the seventeenth century, French traders and Huguenots made colonies in _____ .
         a. India   c. Canada
         b. Japan   d. Mexico

2.012   A good watchword for the Industrial Revolution would be _____ .
         a. Land ho!   c. mother
         b. invention   d. father

2.013   Iron could be manufactured more easily after the discovery of _____ for fuel.
         a. coal   c. hardwood
         b. charcoal   d. electricity

2.014   Textile industries were helped when James Watt invented the _____ .
         a. power mower   c. cotton gin
         b. steam engine   d. submarine

2.015   Besides England, France, Germany, and Belgium, another country involved in the Industrial Revolution was _____ .
         a. the Philippines   c. the United States
         b. Albania   d. Palestine

2.016   A new profession that grew out of the Industrial Revolution was _____ .
         a. marine biologist   c. scientist
         b. medical assistant   d. mechanical engineer

2.017   In order to reach its factories more easily, Britain _____

_____ .

     a. built its factories at the coast
     b. widened and deepened canals
     c. airlifted goods to the harbors
     d. built subways

2.018   To take the lead in the Industrial Revolution, England had enough

_____ .

     a. natural resources   c. space
     b. factory workers   d. men in Parliament

2.019   Martin Luther was at first a _____ .
     a. doctor   c. priest
     b. lawyer   d. farmer

2.020   The man who first invented the telescope was _____ .
     a. Lippershey   c. Gutenberg
     b. Copernicus   d. Erasmus

Complete these statements (each answer, 3 points).

2.021   The man who was both artist and inventor was _____

_____ .

2.022   The scholar who taught that man was able to solve problems for himself was _____ .

2.023   People coming to town to work in factories made the towns _____

_____ .

2.024   Columbus came to America in the year _____ .

2.025   Martin Luther believed a man was saved by _____

_____ .

2.026   Besides being a sculptor and painter, Michelangelo was _____

_____ .

2.027   John Wesley's evangelism helped the people of _____

_____ .

2.028   Cabral discovered _____ .

2.029   The church Calvin founded is the _____
Church.

2.030   What is needed to spin yarn from raw cotton or wool is a _____

_____ .

Answer *true* **or** *false* (each answer, 2 points).

2.031 _____ In the Renaissance all art was about religious subjects.
2.032 _____ Sunday schools had their start during the Industrial Revolution.
2.033 _____ Renaissance artists began to depict the life of the people.

2.034 _____ Luther nailed his ninety-five theses to the door of the castle church at Wittenberg.

2.035 _____ The Gutenberg press made possible the printing of the Bible in the language of the people.

2.036 _____ Robert Raikes invented the spinning jenny.

2.037 _____ Charles Wesley was called "a brand plucked from the burning."

2.038 _____ England's major industry in the early 1800s was textiles.

2.039 _____ Rural life grew in England during the Industrial Revolution.

2.040 _____ England's filthy cities during the Industrial Revolution caused the passage of a Public Health Act.

Answer these questions (each answer, 5 points).

2.041   Describe three inventions that made possible a revolution in the textile industry.

a. _____

_____

b. _____

_____

c. _____

_____

2.042   Name three reasons why England was the country most involved in the Industrial Revolution. _____

_____

_____

_____

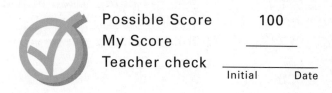

Possible Score   100

My Score   _____

Teacher check   _____

                Initial   Date

III. AGE OF UNREST

Two world wars are the outstanding events of the twentieth century. The most important thing to learn about wars is why they happened. The reasons for World War I were different from the reasons for World War II. You will learn about these reasons and about some things that were done to try to keep peace. You will also learn about two things that have happened since World War II that may have an effect on Europe's future.

SECTION OBJECTIVES

Review these objectives. When you have completed this section, you should be able to:

5. State the starting dates and at least two other facts each about World War I and World War II.

6. Describe the Berlin tragedy.

Restudy these words.

adhere	dictatorship	national socialism
alliance	diplomacy	psychological
apex	extermination	strategy
blockade	fascism	tactics
communism	fascist	unification

REASONS FOR WAR

Many of Western Europe's problems were carried into the twentieth century. Some began as far back as the settlements of the Napoleonic wars in 1815. The men who made the settlements drew boundaries to suit the reigning monarchs. This action left many people with similar nationalities separated from each other. In view of the growing spirit of national pride everywhere, serious problems were created.

Territorial disputes. In efforts to gain back lost territories, military **alliances** were made between countries, that is, they joined together for military help to each other. In 1882 Germany, Austria-Hungary, and Italy formed the Triple Alliance. A Triple *Entente* (understanding) was agreed upon in 1907 between France, Great Britain, and Russia. The effect of these alliances was to divide Western Europe into two camps. The Triple Alliance was set against the Triple Entente.

Serious trouble points existed in three political areas: (1) France wanted to get back its northern province of Alsace-Lorraine from Germany, (2) France was in dispute with Germany over Morocco in North Africa, (3) Serbia wanted to get back from Austria-Hungry two provinces that would give her a seaport. Serbia desired to have better trade with the Middle East.

Colonial expansion. In the meantime, the Industrial Revolution had created new needs. Every country was eager for colonial expansion, mainly for three reasons. Colonies would give a country new products and resources. Competition was fierce for places to invest money. Each country needed far away bases where it could put military supplies and men.

Secret diplomacy. Persons in high places tried to accomplish goals by secret **diplomacy**. Ministers of the same government cabinet often were not told when another minister made an agreement with an outside nation. In those days no international body to settle disputes had been formed. Sometimes all the members of a cabinet knew about an agreement. However, they failed to inform their legislature.

Western Europe was ripe for trouble. The events that followed touched the lives not only of Europeans. Americans and people of all other nations felt the impact, too. You will want to know about these events.

Write on each line what each country wanted.

3.1   France   a. _____
                 b. _____

3.2   Serbia   _____

3.3   Every European country
                 a. _____
                 b. _____
                 c. _____

WORLD WAR I

The date of the start of World War I was June 28, 1914. Archduke Francis Ferdinand, heir to the throne of Austria-Hungary, was visiting in Sarajevo, Bosnia. Bosnia was a province ruled by Austria-Hungary, but was claimed by Serbia. A student from Serbia stepped to the running board of the Archduke Ferdinand's car and killed both the Archduke and his wife. Immediately Austria-Hungary declared war against Serbia. You will learn how many countries became involved in a war that eventually covered all of Europe.

Countries involved. The conflict spread quickly. Germany joined Austria-Hungary because the two countries were in an alliance. The Ottoman Empire (no longer in existence) joined a couple of months later. This group of countries called themselves the Central powers. A year later Bulgaria joined the Central powers.

Before the Armistice was signed in 1918, twenty-four countries, including the United States, had joined together to oppose the Central powers. Allied powers, or Allies, was the name given to this group of countries.

Leaders. Some of the names of men most prominent in World War I were 1) David Lloyd George, prime minister of England; 2) Georges Clemenceau (zhorzh klae mahn soa'), premier of France; 3) Vittorio Orlando, premier of Italy; 4) Czar Nicholas II of Russia; 5) Kaiser (kie' zer) Wilhelm of Germany; 6) Franz Joseph and, later, Charles I, emperors of Austria-Hungary; 7) Woodrow Wilson, President of the United States; 8) General John J. Pershing, an American, Commander of Allied forces in Europe; and 9) Paul von Hindenburg, a German, Commander in Chief of the armies of the Central powers.

War's end. Trenches were dug at roughly four different fronts. At first the Central powers made great gains. Their fronts were established on solid land. In the end, however, the Allies won because of their greater numbers and better resources.

Five million allied men were killed either by wounds or disease. Central powers lost three million servicemen. The war cost more than 337 billion dollars.

In northern France, in a railroad car, the Armistice was signed on November 11, 1918. The Peace Treaty of 1919, at Versailles (ver sie'), near Paris, France, laid the groundwork for the next world war. The total responsibility for World War I was placed on Germany. One-eighth of her territory was taken from her.

Austria and the Ottoman Empire were greatly reduced in size. The countries of Czechoslovakia, Poland, Yugoslavia, and Hungary were formed from territory formerly ruled by other countries.

The world never really stopped fighting. Little combats kept breaking out until 1939.

World War I was mostly fought on land.

Write *true* **or** *false.*

3.4 _____ The date of the start of World War I was June 28, 1944.

3.5 _____ The problems in Europe before World War I dated back to the Roman Empire.

3.6 _____ *Alliance* means *joining together.*

3.7 _____ Serbia wanted a seaport.

3.8 _____ There was no colonial expansion of Western European countries before World War I.

3.9 _____ Secret diplomacy means diplomats meet in dark closets.

3.10 _____ The assassination of Archduke Ferdinand of Austria-Hungary started World War I.

3.11 _____ Germany immediately joined the Allies.

3.12 _____ Winston Churchill led Great Britain in World War I.

3.13 _____ Woodrow Wilson was the World War I President of the United States.

3.14 _____ The Armistice for World War I was signed November 11, 1918.

3.15 _____ In the Peace Treaty, Germany was given total blame for World War I.

REASONS FOR ANOTHER WAR

The groundwork for another war now had been laid. Nevertheless, in the twenty-one years after the Armistice, much talk was heard of ending war forever. In churches and Sunday schools people prayed for peace. Most people honestly hoped that there might be no more war. A League of Nations was formed so that countries would have a place to work out problems without fighting. But political problems, economic depression, and rising **dictatorships** worked together to bring about another world war.

Political problems. Three problems existed in Europe: (1) Much bitterness remained over terms of the Versailles Treaty. (2) Germany had formed itself into a republic, but the republic was weak. No one noticed Germany's awkward attempts to let the people rule themselves. All other countries were too busy building their own democracies to hear Germany's cries for help. Because so much had been taken from Germany after World War I, jobs were very scarce. The people of Germany lost faith and hope. They were ready for a leader who would promise hope. (3) The number of **dictatorships** rose sharply. This should have been offset by the greater rise in democracies. In 1914 only five nations in Europe were republics. By 1932, sixteen nations had formed democratic constitutions. However, the dictatorships made great strides.

The League of Nations. Woodrow Wilson, United States President, dreamed of an international forum for settling disputes. The League of Nations was established in 1920 to promote international cooperation. Most countries involved in World War I joined it. Germany joined too, in a desperate attempt to help herself. The United States never belonged to the League of Nations, even though Woodrow Wilson worked hard for the League. The organization soon lost its effectiveness.

Economic depression. One of the serious aftereffects of World War I was the economic depression of the 1930s. For awhile after the war, money was plentiful. False optimism caused people to spend money carelessly. Eleven years after the Armistice, in 1929, the United States stock market crashed. Bonds and stocks were worthless. The effects of the crash spread all over Western Europe. Huge numbers of people lost their life savings. No resources remained to fall back on. Work was scarce. People who had never needed charity before stood in lines (called "bread lines") to get something to eat from charitable organizations. The moral outlook of the world was shattered.

Dictatorships. The embittered nation of Germany turned to a man who promised hope, Adolf Hitler. His scheme was to rise to power by giving the German people someone else to blame for their troubles. Hitler wrote the declaration of his belief and intentions in a book called *Mein Kampff* (mien komf). His political belief was in **national socialism**. He recommended the use of the military to change the restrictions of the Versailles Treaty. He promised a greater, "purer" Germany by proposing that no Jewish or Slavic people be allowed to marry German people. Hitler also proposed that Germany seize "living room" by force.

The party that helped Hitler rise to power and which he eventually controlled was the Nazi Party. Crushing the Jews and taking territory belonging to other countries, Hitler and the Nazi Party brought prosperity back to Germany. In doing so they stamped out freedom. Austria and Hungary did not resist when the German armies marched in.

In Italy, the **Fascists** took charge. Benito Mussolini (moos' oa lee' nee) appeared on the scene in 1919. By 1922 he had succeeded in being elected prime minister of Italy. He seized all power. He promised what the people wanted to hear. Italy would become a new Rome. The days of the classics would return! Mussolini then captured Albania and Ethiopia.

Russia's Communist Party took over after their revolution in 1917. Under Lenin's leadership, private property was seized. People who disagreed with the government were sent to labor camps in Siberia. After Lenin died, Stalin took over. **Communism** and **fascism** were much alive in Europe during this time.

Japan, in the meantime, was developing a powerful military force. The country's ruler was still the traditional emperor. But the *Samurai* (warrior class) had taken over. They invaded Manchuria in 1931. They had their eyes on winning portions of mainland China. The *Samurai* hoped to rule all of Asia.

Up to this time, Britain, France, and the United States avoided doing much about the aggressions of all these dictators. They wanted to avoid another world war.

Complete one of the following activities.

3.16   Do research on one of these topics and make a written report. Ask your teacher if it is possible to read your report to a group of students.

a. Report on Germany during the time between the two world wars. Look for the reasons that Adolf Hitler was able to become dictator.
b. Report on the League of Nations. Look for the reasons it failed.
c. Report on Italy and the rise to power of Mussolini.
d. Make a report on the economic depression of the 1930s. Interview people who lived through it, if you can. Look for the causes of the depression. Try to find out what the causes were for the return of prosperity.

Teacher check _____

Initial   Date

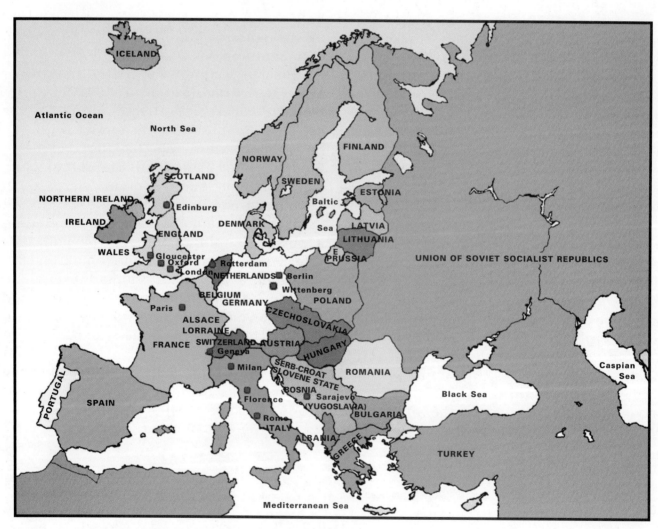

Map 3—Europe as of 1936

That which was feared the most did happen. Germany marched on Poland in September, 1939. This date is the start of the Second World War. Before it was over, battlegrounds involved Asia, Europe, North Africa, and the Atlantic and Pacific Oceans.

You will learn of the wide scope of World War II. Nearly everyone, everywhere was involved in it, perhaps even your parents or grandparents. Many persons in Europe still have deep problems that resulted from World War II.

Countries involved. France and Britain took immediate steps to stop Germany when Germany invaded Poland. As soon as France and Britain declared war, Germany recruited five other European countries. These countries called themselves the Axis powers. The Axis powers included Italy, Hungary, Romania, Bulgaria, and Finland. Japan joined the Axis in December of 1941. Russia was an Axis country until June, 1941, when Germany invaded Russia.

France could not help England for long. Soon after the declaration of war, Hitler moved across Denmark, Norway, Holland, Belgium, and France. All of these countries were occupied by the Nazis.

Gradually, England gathered other help. The Allies, or Allied powers, came to include almost all of the other countries in the world except the few Axis nations. By the war's end, the entire globe was involved one way or another—even the few neutral countries. For World War II, however, the "Big Four" Allied powers were China, Russia, Great Britain, and the United States. Russia fought on the Allied side toward the end of the war.

In the first years of the war, the United States provided money and supplies to the European Allies, but for two years it stayed out of the war. Then on December 7, 1941, Japan attacked Pearl Harbor, Hawaii, by air. Much damage was done to American warships that day. The reason for Japan's attack was simple. Japan wanted access to the islands of the Pacific. The Japanese believed that if they destroyed the United States' Pacific fleet, they would have no interference in their plans.

War on Japan was immediately declared by the United States. This declaration automatically involved the United States in the European war, too. We sent ships, men, and supplies to both Europe and the Pacific. For the most part, men went to war willingly. Clearly our cherished democracy was again threatened.

Features. Much of World War II was won by aerial attack. The German word *blitzkrieg* (blitz' kreeg) was familiar to everyone. It meant *lightning war*. Enemy bombings from the air were fast and furious. Beautiful old cities were all but destroyed in a few hours. Blitzkrieg **tactics** reached an **apex** when the United States used atomic bombs over Hiroshima (he roa she' ma or he roa' she ma) and Nagasaki (na ga sa' kee) in Japan. The world abruptly learned the strength of atomic power.

Another tactic used by the Germans was **extermination**. Adolf Hitler thought only Aryan (pure-blood white) people should be citizens of Germany. He killed as many Jewish persons as he could.

The Allied powers depended on **strategy**. Aircraft, ships at sea, and ground forces worked together. By 1942 England and the United States had combined their Chiefs of Staff. Together they worked out movements such as "D-day." On "D-day," June 6, 1944, the combined air, ground, and sea personnel crossed the English Channel. All of these forces entered mainland Europe at Normandy, France. They began immediately to push the German forces back out of France and the Lowlands. Within a year the war in Europe was ended.

Other tactics used in this war, the greatest war, were (1) espionage (es' pee uh noj) or spying; (2) **psychological** warfare—enemies tried hard to play tricks on the minds of the soldiers (by loud speaker systems, radio broadcasts, and printed material); and (3) underground activity (secretly helping soldiers and civilians to outwit the enemy was common).

Leaders. Of course a war as large as World War II had many leaders. Most of them will not be mentioned here. You have learned about Lenin, Stalin, Mussolini, and Hitler. The Commander-in-Chief of the Allied Forces was General Dwight David Eisenhower. He later became the thirty-fourth President of the United States. General Douglas MacArthur commanded the Pacific forces.

The United States President during the war was Franklin D. Roosevelt. Upon the death of Roosevelt, Harry Truman became President. In England Winston Churchill and Clement Attlee were prime ministers.

Wars end. May 8, 1945, was "V-E Day" (Victory in Europe) in the European War. Germany surrendered five years, eight months, and seven days after it invaded Poland.

A peace treaty in Europe has never been signed, but peace agreements have been **adhered** to. Germany was divided into four sections. Control of one section each was granted to Great Britain, France, Russia, and the United States. The parts allotted to England, France, and the United States were, in effect, given back to Germany under supervision. This combined nation was called West Germany. Russia took its portion and made it a part of its Communist Block. This portion was East Germany.

Japan surrendered on August 10, 1945. The peace treaty gradually returned her powers. By 1952, Japan had regained full national position.

China, one of the Big Four, had no part in the European agreements. Four years after Japan surrendered, Communists took over mainland China, forcing the Chinese Nationalists (Allies in World War II) to the Island of Taiwan.

Make the following lists. Use material in the paragraphs you have just read.

3.17   List the European Axis powers in World War II.

a. _____   d. _____

b. _____   e. _____

c. _____   f. _____

3.18   List four methods of warfare employed in this war.

a. _____   c. _____

b. _____   d. _____

3.19   List three of the problems in Europe that led up to World War II.

a. _____

b. _____

c. _____

38

3.20   List the European countries that had dictatorships, name the dictator, and name the kind of political belief.

   a. _____

   b. _____

   c. _____

3.21   List the first countries Germany captured after World War II was declared.

   a. _____   c. _____

   b. _____   d. _____

3.22   List the four countries that received control of portions of Germany after World War II.

   a. _____   c. _____

   b. _____   d. _____

3.23   List the "Big Four" Allied powers in World War II.

   a. _____   c. _____

   b. _____   d. _____

YEARS AFTER WORLD WAR II

More has happened in modern Europe than you have time to study in this LIFEPAC. Two events are of special importance. The formation of the United Nations is important because it was an attempt to do what the League of Nations failed to do—keep the peace. The other event you will study is the tragedy of the division of the city of Berlin. Read thoughtfully, because the kinds of decisions that are made by adults today will be made by you when you reach voting age.

The United Nations. Shortly after the Japanese attack on Pearl Harbor, twenty-six countries met together. The place was San Francisco, Ca. The date was January, 1942. These delegates signed a Declaration of Intent to form another international body. They planned to call it the United Nations. Much doubt surrounded this movement because of the failure of the League of Nations, but much hope existed, too.

In San Francisco, from April to June, 1945, the charter for the United Nations was drafted. Fifty participating countries signed it. The United States became a member this time. The charter became valid in October, 1945.

The United Nations has General Assembly sessions in which delegates from all over the world sit together to discuss problems. Besides this, departments for agriculture exist, as well as for world money problems, world health, and civil aviation. The department for the welfare of the world's children is called UNICEF.

The Berlin tragedy. The city of Berlin was the proud capital of all Germany. You have learned how the country of Germany was divided after World War II. The division put Berlin deep inside the Soviet (Russian) zone of East Germany.

By postwar agreement, the city of Berlin was divided in the same four parts that Germany was. France, England, and the United States allowed West Berlin the freedom of self-government, under supervision. Russia isolated her portion of the city, which was referred to as East Berlin. East Berlin was the capital of East Germany. The two nations remained divided until 1990.

You may find Berlin's experience with communism frightening, but you should be aware of it. Perhaps you will understand better the importance it may be in future years to guard your own city and country from dictatorships.

In 1948 Soviet Russia **blockaded** all ground traffic from West Germany to West Berlin. This blockade made the famous Berlin Airlift necessary. Airlift was the only way goods, services, and people could reach West Berlin. It continued for almost a year. The planes had to fly on a certain line of flight ordered by Russian officials. This line of flight was called the Berlin Corridor.

After the blockade two highways led from West Germany to West Berlin. Tourists could not leave either highway. Warnings were given drivers to start their journey with a full tank of gas.

By 1961 the Soviets had begun to worry about the thousands of persons who were crossing every year from East Berlin to free West Berlin. (This included many elderly people who had permission.) Therefore, they built a high dividing wall along the line that separated the two parts of the city. Even the windows on the East German side of the wall were concreted. Barbed wire covered the barriers. Guards watched day and night.

Berlin's tragedy, then, was that it was divided by the Soviets from part of its mother country. Also it was divided within itself. Imagine, if you can, a high, guarded wall built down the main street of your town or city! This wall remained in place for about 28 years. In that time many prayers were lifted for the German people.

You may want to read Mark chapter 13. Here Jesus predicts many trials that will come to earth's people. Problems of today often seem much like those that Jesus describes. Similar readings can be found

The Berlin Wall was built in 1961.

in Matthew chapter 24 and Luke chapter 21. These passages record what is called the "Olivet discourse." Jesus was telling his disciples that He will come again when we least expect it. He advises us to go about our daily business. His command is (Mark 13:33), "Take ye heed, watch and pray..." By the end of the 1980s, Communism was beginning to fail in East Germany. On November 9, 1989, the East German government opened the border to West Germany. The Berlin Wall was destroyed. **Unification** talks began between the United States, France, England, the USSR, and East and West German officials. One thing agreed upon was that the new Germany would not make any atom bombs. In 1990 the two Germanys merged and on December 20, 1990, an all-German election was held. Germany is now a Federal Republic. Helmut Kohl, the first Chancellor of Germany, was re-elected in 1994.

Complete these activities.

3.24 Write in full sentences your explanation of the Berlin tragedy. Why is it no longer a problem?

_____

_____

_____

_____

3.25 Imagine a line drawn down the middle of your city or town. Put this line on the main street, as far as the street stretches. Write, or make a list, of places you could not go, or people you could not see, if you were not allowed to cross this line. What will help prevent this happening again anywhere?

_____

_____

_____

Complete these lists.

3.26 List the original Axis countries

a. _____   e. _____

b. _____   f. _____

c. _____   g. _____

d. _____   h. _____

3.27 List the Allied powers.

a. _____   d. _____

b. _____   e. _____

c. _____

Complete this map study on Map 3 on page 36 of the LIFEPAC.

3.28 a. Color the European Axis countries yellow.
b. Color the European Allied countries green.

Before you take this last Self Test, you may want to do one or more of these self checks.

1. _____ Read the objectives. See if you can do them.
2. _____ Restudy the material related to any objectives that you cannot do.
3. _____ Use the SQ3R study procedure to review the material:
   a. **S**can the sections.
   b. **Q**uestion yourself.
   c. **R**ead to answer your questions.
   d. **R**ecite the answers to yourself.
   e. **R**eview areas you did not understand.
4. _____ Review all vocabulary, activities, and Self Tests, writing a correct answer for every wrong answer.

SELF TEST 3

Write the correct letter and answer on each line (each answer, 2 points).

3.01 Serbia wanted _____ .
   a. industry   c. a seaport
   b. East Europe   d. an airfield

3.02 When ministers in a government cabinet fail to tell their fellow ministers about agreements they have made, this action is called

   _____ .

   a. secret diplomacy   c. cold war
   b. clever negotiation d. a rotten trick

3.03 The year World War I started was _____ .
   a. 1910   c. 1939
   b. 1914   d. 1929

3.04 The United States never joined the _____ .
   a. Allies   c. United Nations
   b. League of Nations d. Pacific command

3.05 Adolf Hitler was the head of the _____ .
   a. German Nazis   c. Russian Communists
   b. Italian Fascists   d. Japanese military

3.06 World War II started in _____ .
   a. 1939   c. 1945
   b. 1914   d. 1918

3.07   The Commander-in-Chief of the Allied Forces in World War II was

_____ .

a.   General Pershing   c.   President Wilson
b.   General Eisenhower

3.08   Decisive features in fighting World War II were _____

_____ .

a.   air blitzes and strategy   c.   trenches and tanks
b.   democracy plus bravery   d.   the many undergrounds

3.09   The event that triggered World War I was _____

_____ .

a.   trouble in Morocco   c.   the murder of Archduke Ferdinand
b.   renewed secret diplomacy   d.   Alsace-Lorraine

3.010   The international forum today is the _____ .
a.   Monroe Doctrine   c.   United Nations
b.   NATO   d.   League of Nations

Write the correct answer on each line (each answer, 3 points).

3.011   When the stock market failed in the United States, it threw all of Europe
into an economic _____ .

3.012   After World War II, France, England, the United States, and Russia
divided _____ among them.

3.013   The ceilings of Renaissance churches were _____
by the Renaissance architects.

3.014   The geographical area of Europe that is separated from the rest of
Europe by water is _____ .

3.015   Charles Wesley wrote _____ .

3.016   Iron manufacture was helped by the discovery of _____
for fuel.

3.017   England had better and more _____ resources for leading
the industrial Revolution.

3.018   Petrarch and Erasmus were part of the awakening in the area of

_____ .

3.019   The word *Renaissance* means _____ .

3.020   In order to come out of the Dark Ages, most early scholars thought the
world had to return to _____ .

Match the following words and phrases (each answer, 2 points).

3.021 _____ the Last Supper

3.022 _____ around the world

3.023 _____ Luther's teachings

3.024 _____ textile manufacture

3.025 _____ the scientific method

3.026 _____ Magna Carta

3.027 _____ *blitzkrieg*

3.028 _____ Huguenots

3.029 _____ Erasmus

3.030 _____ Calvin

a. England's main industry during eighteenth and nineteenth centuries
b. Kaiser Wilhelm
c. the attempt in the thirteenth century to gain power for the people
d. Leonardo da Vinci
e. lightning war
f. one of Magellan's ships
g. French Protestants
h. theologian in Geneva
i. first-century Christianity
j. Catholic scholar
k. the way scientists gain and store knowledge

Answer these questions (each answer, 3 points).

3.031 What kind of political belief did Hitler have? _____

3.032 What kind of political belief did Mussolini have? _____

3.033 What kind of political belief did Lenin have? _____

3.034 What did Hitler, Mussolini, and Lenin have in common? _____

3.035 What is a dictator? _____

Complete these activities (each answer, 5 points).

3.036   Explain the Berlin tragedy in your own words. _____

_____

_____

_____

_____

3.037   Name two major steps in textile manufacturing. _____

_____

3.038   Tell in your own words how a Christian can approach God. _____

_____

_____

_____

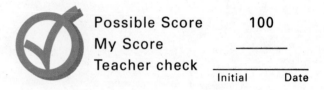

Possible Score	100
My Score	_____
Teacher check	_____
	Initial Date

Before taking the LIFEPAC Test, you may want to do one or more of these self checks.

1. _____   Read the objectives. See if you can do them.
2. _____   Restudy the material related to any objectives that you cannot do.
3. _____   Use the SQ3R study procedure to review the material.
4. _____   Review activities, Self Tests, and LIFEPAC vocabulary words.
5. _____   Restudy areas of weakness indicated by the last Self Test.